Randoms

Ariel Hampton

BookLeaf Publishing

India | USA | UK

Presentation by *BookLeaf Publishing*

Web: www.bookleafpub.com

E-mail: info@bookleafpub.com

ISBN: 978-93-5744-345-6

First edition 2022

ACKNOWLEDGEMENT

If it wasn't for my church, family, and friends I wouldn't have anything to write about. I especially would like to thank my mom who actually thinks me being an artist is better than being that pharmacist I promised her I'll be.

PREFACE

When I write it can get real bloody.
I always hated my emotional spills.

Survivor

What a torture when He allowed me to open my
eyes
My dreams kept me from being thankful
It prepared this grave I couldn't pull from
Though it was built off of silence and seclusion
The best part was being sealed

Transitions

We are no longer blossoming under full moons
anymore
But by the sun rays that pour on us like honey
And gives us a glisten like the morning dew

The Phoenix

Her soul was dipped in gold and her body
shimmered
like crystals laughing in the sky
She was the fulfillment of a prayer
that was spoken from careful thought
and manifested in the pit of the hearts vault
No man nor nature could tame the wild in this
divine child
For she belonged to the Son
whose rays gave her sweet radiation
And when she's done her ashes fall to the ground
like snow
Evidence of this old creature run with the wind
but out of the dust comes this new divinity
A woman not of myth
But a living sculpture of love from the Potter's
hands

Night Terrors

As i submerged in the quiet moonlight
I noticed the earth's silence
but God was not still
My pain kept glowing
My flaws could not stop showing
and every thought became real
He knew i was worried, anxious, and scared
yet God kept moving
He kept working wonders still

Dream Blocks

And there is no doubt that my brain is fried
from that constant back and forth stumbling
Why can't I pull from this mindless sorcery?
You know like the ritual the moon does with the
tides
The more I pulled away the more monsters came
from behind
I'll just be glad when I can get away
Away from my own mind.

Butterflies in a jar

They are still giving us this image of being
American
while bottling the pursuit of our dreams
I'm so tired of dreaming for freedom from afar
I'm so tired of living like a butterfly in a jar
No hope, no future, and just living by any means

B.B.B

Waning through your words
like when the moon goes through a phase
But you kind of give me a resistance
like being hypnotized without the daze
I could follow you for days and listen to you for
hours
Your words turn into living flowers
And you're feeding me food that I never knew
Now when I look in the mirror my image blurs
right into you
What is in me is in you too
Beautiful Brown Boy

Morning Sickness

I woke up insane this morning….
Anxiety gripped tight like a noose around my
neck
As I sat rocking and waiting through my
existence
I suffered through this affliction
Wasted in this cult of depression
And the leader is so surreptitious
He zipped a mad man in the sweetest frame
And that's when I knew I was deranged
When all of my solutions ended up building a
grave

Love is the New Black

I like where I'm going
The steps are so crystal clear
Pity me for thinking
to end it all right here
Now I gotta purpose
and heavy is the task
I look at me and then I see
Love is the new black

Reality Check

Just thinking back how I was stupid and
dedicated to the wrong things
like being dedicated to a human being
Forgetting things that are important
Like for one I serve a jealous God
You can't serve God and serve a thing
and if you choose wrong you lost Everything
Now I'm careful to what I give my time to
You couldn't pay me to do what I use too

Silent was the Killer

I never was the type to talk about a lot of terrible
things...
Now that I am older
I realized that's a terrible thing
A quite but sweet composure
but inside I've slid through some terrible things
And when I couldn't hold it I told it
You know people say the most terrible things

A rose in the dark

I really hate talking to people
I'd rather just talk to myself
I'd rather just give it to God
He really the G.O.A.T with the help
I could've shot help in my veins
I could've slit help on my wrist
I could've popped help with some pills
I just thank God that I exist
And you might not take this seriously
But I thank God that I'm here
If you could see what was killing me
You would thank God that I'm here
Don't ever think I'm talking figuratively
When I thank God that I'm here

HIM

It was nothing serious
He made me laugh
From time to time we'll link and watch some
anime
Go sit, chat, and drink green tea
And talk about why people are not reading now
a days
He was really weird but he was fit for it
We would read the Bible so I guess he had the
sense
Never had to think twice about the way he
moved
Never had to question any of his intent
He didn't believe in straddling the fence
Whatever he said he believed in his word
 A lot of his words aligned with his actions
 And how hard it is to find someone to prove by
their actions
Conversations included wealth and not just
monetary
We would exchange thoughts on things that kept
us in our own oppression
What I liked most he spoke very much about
change

We really wanted things to change
So we started to change ourselves
And we started to better ourselves
We promised to give more love and to never
judge but help our people instead
In all honesty we were just tired of our own
being misled

Grace

As my mind started to pace
I started to feel the zing from the sun rays
Form there I had to stop and say
"Thank you Lord"
I saw how the grass is so green
And how beautifully positioned was each tree
Again, I stopped and said
"Thank you Lord"
Looked at the birds in the sky and
For a minute so was I
In awe I stopped and said
"Thank you Lord"
Last night I cried and cried
moaned and rocked side to side
Though He says weeping may endure for a night
It was guaranteed that joy came dancing with the
sunrise
With so much grace
I turned up my face and said
"Thank you Lord"
My rock and soul sustainer

Bare

In a mature way he aroused my mind
His words were more than roses on the bed and
red wine
Before I knew it I was out of my clothes
Not materially but my soul
Naked and bare he saw every bit of me
This man unclothed me emotionally
I knew then that this was more than a sexual
healing
but a revealing that a man couldn't touch a
woman physically without touching her feelings

All night blues

Eyes blood red
Used so many tissues
caused a slight nosebleed
All the things I buried won't stop bothering me
Heavy contemplations overdosing strong
sedatives
Living through a revelation
Asking God to give me patience
drained from all the waiting
why is waiting underrated?
I had to learn my time is not aligned with the
Creator
wished I learned this lesson sooner
my heart's a mess, a defect that comes with
being human

Psalms in the Valley I

The enemy delights in my trouble
but the Lord brings comfort in my distress
The same God who walked in the shadows of
death with David
is the same God that will prepare my table today.
when I cried the Lord listened
when i hungered the Lord gave bread
Solid is his position
and mighty is His hand
and in this I will praise the Lord
I will rejoice always in thine presence
For the God I serve lives!
and His mercy endureth forever!
Praise be to my rock!
The foundation of my salvation!

Psalms In The Valley II

I asked and He answered
How considerate our God is He!
From fear came the knowledge , Oh how God
teaches me!
How to walk and how to talk
He shows how love is supposed to be
and I'm promised a crown when the world falls
down if I just do the right things

Shrooms

I'd be in denial if I said I like to smile
Love songs make me gag
Suicide letters are just love notes
When I wanna talk to the dead
When you see me happy just let me be
I'm caught up in a trance
No ritual but spiritual, makes me feel invisible
Moves the grim right out of my head
Torture is a high
Gory gets me in the mood
I'll wear black in the sunlight
If blood could be perfume
But once this trance gets to me
My demons dare not come out
It's light is bright and will put up a fight
To keep my my mind from going down

I need you

Yes I want my space
but I want you right there
Don't go no where
Stay by me
Yes i love my space
but you are right there
You could be anywhere
but you stay by me

The Fountain

Heavy are the feet that are broken
but light is the heart that forgives
Lay me at the fountain of fresh and cooling
water
where dead things now live
There is a fountain full of streams that flows
through Emmanuels veins
with water so pure and healed afflictions that
time couldn't
The rainbows danced with permission
while angels prepared my joyful admission
And as I emerged from this fountain
He celebrated my renewing
He welcomed my change of a new being
and I will forever go to this fountain
where peace, love, and wholeness can be found
and life has no ending